ZERO TO TEN

First published in Australia by Five Mile Press
67 Rushdale Street, Knoxfield, Victoria 3180 Australia

Published in Great Britain in 1999 by Zero to Ten Limited,
46 Chalvey Road East, Slough, Berkshire SL1 2LR

A CIP catalogue record for this book is available from the British Library.

ISBN 1-84089-129-7

Printed and bound in Singapore

A FIRST BOOK ABOUT SCIENCE

It's Much Too Hot!

BOB GRAHAM

It's much too hot.
Look at the flowers.

It’s too hot for dogs.
Look at Patch’s tongue.

And it's too hot for Jenny.
Look at her mop her wet brow.

There is only one place for Patch.

It's cooler in the shade of a tree.

Jenny's feet are hot and sticky.
Look how pink they are.

There is only one thing to
do with feet like that.

There is only one thing to do with the garden hose.

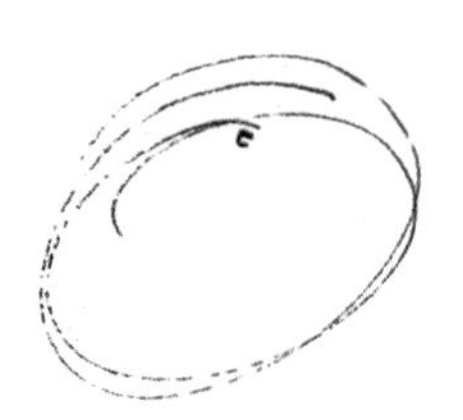

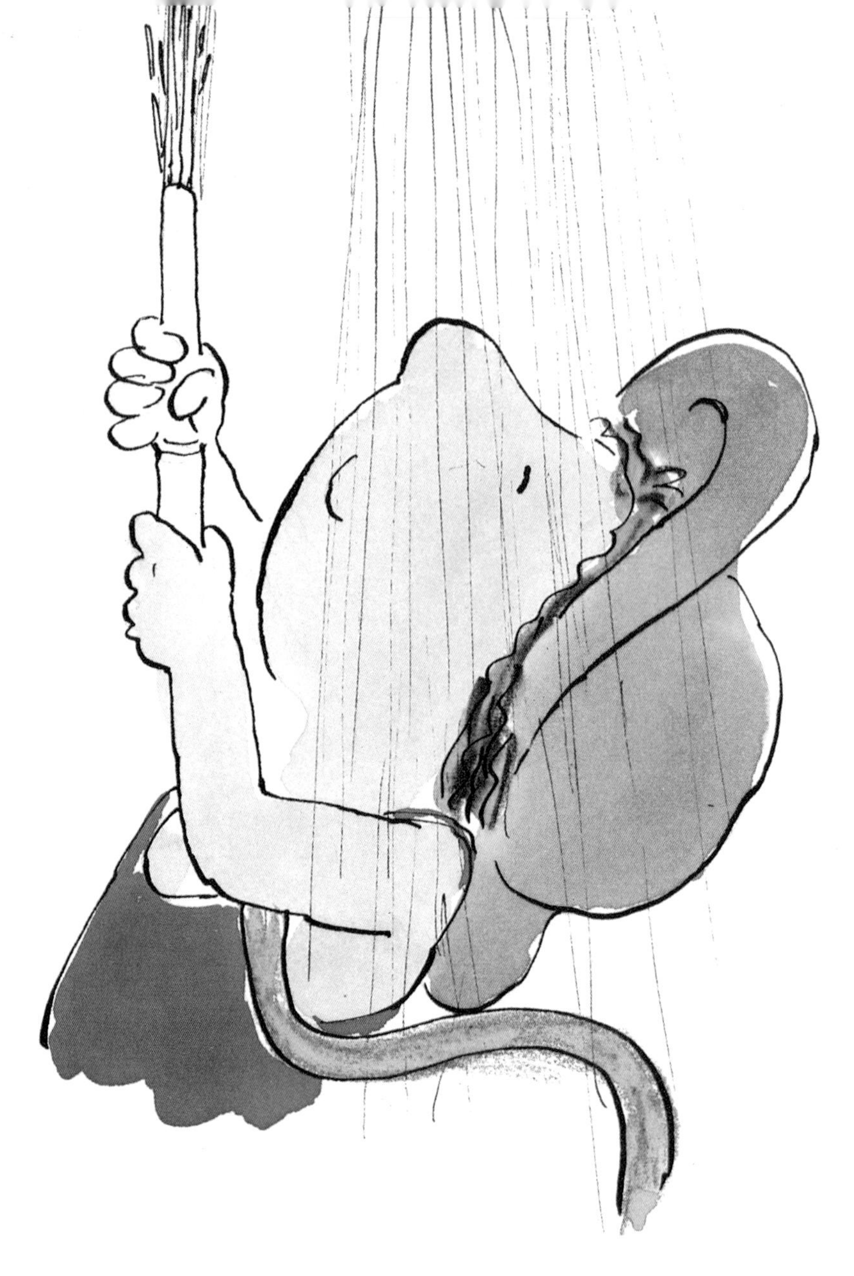

Jenny feels much cooler.

Her droopy flowers may soon
feel better too.

When Jenny stops watering,
the heat will dry the puddles.

Jenny is looking for things to water.
Patch will find another cool shadow.

He does not like water games.

When the sun goes down . . .

. . . it will be much cooler.

Background Notes for Parents and Teachers

Everything around us is made up of tiny pieces called particles. The particles in solid things, such as rock or wood, are joined together densely and tightly. The particles in liquids, such as water, are spread out loosely. And the particles in gases, such as air, are spread even further apart.

Heat can change the way these particles are joined together. For example, when water is heated, the particles move further and further apart until they turn into a gas called water vapour. This process is called evaporation.

Experiments to try with children

1. Outline a puddle in chalk and, after about 10 minutes, make another outline to see how much water has evaporated.

2. Place a mixture of water and salt in a saucer and leave in the sun. What is left when the water evaporates?

3. Time how long it takes for a block of ice to melt:
   a) in the sun
   b) in the shade